PASSION

David Morley is an ecologist and naturalist by background. He studied Zoology at the University of Bristol and pursued research on acid rain. His awards for poetry include the Ted Hughes Award and a Cholmondeley Award. His last poetry collection *FURY* was a Poetry Book Society Choice and shortlisted for the Forward Prize for Best Collection. David is a Professor of Creative Writing at Warwick University and a Fellow of The Royal Society of Literature.

PASSION

DAVID MORLEY

CARCANET POETRY

First published in Great Britain in 2025 by
Carcanet
Alliance House, 30 Cross Street
Manchester, M2 7AQ
www.carcanet.co.uk

A CIP catalogue record for this book is
available from the British Library.

ISBN 978 1 80017 481 8

Book design by Andrew Latimer, Carcanet
Typesetting by LiteBook Prepress Services
Printed in Great Britain by SRP Ltd, Exeter, Devon

The publisher acknowledges financial
assistance from Arts Council England.

CONTENTS

The work of the eyes is done.
Go now and do the heart-work on
the images imprisoned within you.

RAINER MARIA RILKE

To Siobhan

THE MIST NET RELEASES HER BIRDS

You open a window to the morning mist of this ghazal.
I release songbirds from the mist net of this ghazal.

You write to me from Morocco. Your messages migrate from midnight.
They fly in fabled feathers towards gables of this ghazal.

A pandemic makes prisoners of us. I reach out to you
across Spain and the Bay of Biscay from this ghazal.

Swifts swoop over Sahara. Our postcards crisscross a world.
What birds could we be, flowing through this ghazal?

Morning sings with landfall, overhears swallows over oases,
the Mediterranean murmurating in this ghazal.

You watch an acacia and oak fly past your train's window.
Their leaf-tips unfurl in the forest of this ghazal.

'It is strange that the sounds of nature are never heard,' you say.
Silence surrounds the singing glades of this ghazal.

'We resist through poetry,' you write, 'poems are a kind
of politics as well as religion.' Pray kindly for this ghazal.

A Saharan *djinn* twists in a sirocco of words.
Your lines spin twinned between voices of this ghazal

and our voices twine around its lines.
Open the mist net. Throw wide the wings of this ghazal.

a thought. —
hold it —
unrehearsed
dreamed on to the stage
of the flower's mouth
as if she were an actor
called from the wings
of the theatre of flowers
with no time
to take breath:
the spotlight
of the corolla hunts her
like a searchlight
on the glisten and
rainbows of plumage
(the fewest number
of feathers on any bird)
as she havers
in the hover of
the time warp of her
wingbeats, her speech
of nanoseconds:
her nectar.
and moment.

RINGING SWALLOWS

Swallows clip the lake for a sip of water,
or kerfuffle their feathers as they dip for a bathe.
They stipple ellipses across the surface like a skimming stone.
None skitter the water except by glitch or error
nor overwinter under its ice-barred door.

When swallows vanished into September
we thought them depth-bound, cold, deaf as flatfish
slumbering in the benthos until April unleashed them
in whirlpooling flocks with vortices of mayfly
to cram their chicks' clamorous gapes.

In 1740 Johann Leonhard Frisch
wound wool to the legs of swallow chicks.
When the air-streaming birds swooped home to their nests in spring
the threads had not cast their colour
nor the swallows their rings.

BABY BIRDS

Spring has weighed and measured her fledglings
on scales of light and the flight of dark.

To the guillemots nesting on Vestmanna, she says,
your jumplings will not plummet in the morning.

Absolved, too, are the shock-headed herons
squabbling over the broken crowns

of their heronry shipwrecked on crosstrees.
And the pufflings and storm petrels deep

in the long pockets of their burrows, asleep
under rocks and stones and storms

with the eye of the Atlantic watching.

And blessed also is the eaglet, tiptoeing
the edge of her eyrie on a tightrope of air.

Pardoned are the owlets and the eyas
staring saucepan-eyed from nest holes.

Acquitted too are pipits in nest cups,
and tomtits in birdhouses, popping

their heads out like jacks from their boxes.
Spring has weighed and measured her birds

by the flight of the dark on scales of light.

A SKYLARK SLOWED DOWN TO SYLLABLES

When I died, I woke
to a skylark song
slowed down to syllables.

Not the human-heard
fervour of notes
fireworking
from its throat.

I heard it as bird.
Its true sound.
A speech of spirals.
How a lark hears a lark.

His voice resounded
in spheres in spheres in spheres
above, beyond, and down
the meadows and towns.

Another lark, skying,
caught his song, bodied
heavenward in a being
so rapider than my own
until the birds vanished,

no sound but their song
intertwining
into the one longing,
where everything
slowed to the truth.

PUFFINS ON BARDSEY

for Gabriel

beak-clasped catch
    of a clupeoid—
        the puffins skittering
           across the glitter

swivelling between
    tines of their wingtips
        over waves that slip,
           flipped down the air's

tipped stairs to their
    shearwater-scrounged
        burrows, where their
           pufflings gasp underground,

all frizz and fluff-crowns:
    rug-headed kerns,
        clemmed, clumping
           up a skerry of sky

from their coney-warm,
    shearwatered earths,
        gawping and gaping for
           silver shivers of sand-eels

prised from the purse
    of their parents'
        clamped closed, clown-
           daubed beaks.

HELIGOLAND TRAP ON SKOKHOLM ISLAND

An
Alder
Flycatcher
survived a gale
then a storm. Starved,
wind-hurled out of his senses,
he flickered into our Heligoland trap
where we bagged him with a Firecrest
and a hopping mad Chough. The Flycatcher
is the star, a gnat-master from Alaska
of the *tyrant* genus, the double-
peaked caller with the
kitter-call.

We lay out the ringing pliers and needle-nose pliers.

I hatch
the bird from
my bare hands
into the warden's palm.
Her deft bird-ringer's grip
clasps the Flycatcher's nape
between finger and thumb with
a strength just less than caress. She
whispers the biometric data: chord
measurements, wing ratios, the
Flycatcher's mass no more
than a breathing out
of the Atlantic.

THE CUPCAKE METHOD FOR
WEIGHING STORM PETREL CHICKS

*On The Faroe Islands, researchers place a petrel chick in a
paper baking case to weigh it*

for Edward

Storm Petrel chicks are soft and fluffy
with a plush velvety crumb,
infused with elegant buttery flavours
perfectly shaped with a golden dome,
much more tender and aerier than
your run-of-the-mill Storm Petrels,
less cloying, more likely to rise.
And they stay fresh for four days.

Keep them at room temperature,
not fridge cold. This is the key to make
the chick extraordinarily light and fluffy
and you will not get an eggy flavour.
Warm them through but do not overdo.
The birds will emerge effortlessly
with a firm but gentle pressure
and seem to weigh almost nothing.

Their sweetness will take your breath away.

WE MAKE MANX SHEARWATERS VOMIT BOTTLECAPS

'Here is what a stomach full of plastic
looks like,' says the bird reserve warden.
'You can see it stretched so much that the shapes
of plastic are visible. When I say we make
shearwaters vomit bottle caps I'm not exaggerating.'
He twists the dead Manxie on its back,
snipping the sac open. His forceps fossick
into the dissected bird. Rubbish piles up
by the body. I try to focus on the wing feathers.

Eye-bright and gliding over wave crests
the shearwater rides on updraught and jetstream.
A placid sea is her unploughed field.
The bird bends on the blade of storm to turn
the seabed over, drive deep swells to the surface.
The wind swings north, the moon's gravity
tilts the sea-surge. For phytoplankton this
is everything life needs, and they flicker
and breed in that frenzy of crosscurrents
the fish following the glut of plankton
dumped on the surface like data
from the dark. The shearwater's compass
stills, she stabs straight into the undertow
where her fish-prey spiral in their bait-ball
like an underwater galaxy, a million stars
spawning in a nebula of bioluminescence.

The warden stares up at me: 'Don't look away.'

This is what a poem full of plastic looks like.

SKY
   SKYLA
      spéirling
      laverock
      põldlõoke
      Sanglerke
     skowronek
     sönglævirki
     lauku cirulis
      skrivàn polní
       alosa communes
       himmellærke
       Veldleeuwerik
        mezei pacsirta
        dirvinis vieversys
        alouette de champs
         cherêsko gilabayitóri
        škovránok polný
        alondra común
       poljski škrjane
       Feldlerche
       sånglärka
       Ehedydd
       allodola
        zemuta
         laverca
          uiseag
           speur
             kiuru
              EARTH

PRAYER

pray,
what distinguishes one
moth from another?
the time-carved characteristic
of *orthosia gothica*
is a sable etching
on the nub of her forewing.
the figure tells between
this moth and her sisters
that rest with wings tilted
above them like tents.
the edges of her wings
are pommelled embers.
she alights from saxifrage
and solomon's seal
flickering through April
and June between
sun's thorn and moon's
flower; secretes scent-
tails, perfumes for
courtiers, her night-
flight trailing
pheromones, contrails.
all night, she prays
with her wings
held wide
to the hard flames
of headlights.

MOSQUITO

your territory is skin.
you bide your moment,
wiping the windows
of your compound eyes
with your forelegs
feigning to be nothing.
you calculate one
fraction of epidermis
from a thousand fractals.
your tarsus and tibia
are angled to sly.
your palp and proboscis
taste-test the air.
you assemble yourselves
on unapproachable precipices
in holding patterns
of accomplices.
at dusk, you do not flit.
you *ghost*.
your halters fire up
in silence. your wings
are state secrets.
your stealth swerves
the piccolo echoes
of pipistrelles.
few humans are fly
enough to swat you.
you make three wishes
with your proboscis
before settling to it.
most don't see you
or sense you suckle.
we cannot hide.
there is no mercy.

ZOOPLANKTON

These are our stories, and *these are our stories*
—say the protists,
nanoplanktonic flagellates,
cnidarians, ctenophores,
rotifers, chaetognatha,
veliger larvae, copepods,
cladocera, euphausids,
krill and tunicates,
blooming under
the swell of waves
in shoals of
star and moonlight,
alphabeting into
bioluminescence
down the world's
water columns.
These were our stories, and *these were our stories*
—sigh the waveforms
lost in their telling
over oceans over oceans.

HYPHAE

Filaments of fungi intertwine with the tips of tree roots to form underground networks.

A thing was so shameful
I buried it for years.
Twenty years
of sun and snow.
It would not grow.
I let it flame or freeze.
Then I thought
to tend it, see
if it might thrive
if warmed by
forgiveness. I dug
into my heart
and found it
had grown, but
grown down,
shimmering
like hyphae
into the deep
and subdividing
darkness underground.

SWANS

Index to Flamsteed's Observations of the Fixed Stars by Caroline Herschel, 1798

Caroline Herschel turns her telescope
on her first comet, its swan's neck of snow

dipping into the dark water of space.
The curved tine of its tail trailing, flickering

signalling for a likeness of light
among the nebulae and unbroken night

where two swans of ice might sweep
the perihelion in parallel parabolas

of double stars and orbiting pairs.
Caroline steadies her focus. The polished lens

of her Newtonian reflector
light-gathers the flight of every star.

The swans have flown, brother and sister.

They named the first comet after her.

THE FIRST BOOK PRINTED BY THE SUN
*Photographs of British Algae: Cyanotype Impressions by
Anna Atkins, 1843*

Anna Atkins presses dried seaweed on paper:
Corynephora, Catanella, Laminaria.

Sunlight sears their images for an hour.
She spells out the specimens in algal fibres,

fretting them on the ferric coated paper.
Anna washes the light-burned pictures in water.

The rockpools of pages, where the sea rolls in
as her eye passes over them like the moon

and her seaweeds wave in star-startled wonder
as the tide of her hands lifts them one by one

Sargassum, Phyllophora, Punctaria,
into the first book printed by the sun.

ODE TO A NIGHTINGALE

I clip an angel's wing and unweave rainbows.
The spectra are alight with star-flung fires.
God's geometry knows no number.
A pterodactyl is his trigonometry in flight.
Fossil finds are an annal of lies, you claim.
I say, the fossil record is an alphabet of light.
Eukaryotic cells are Eros and Psyche.
Nature is Mozart to God's Salieri.
We sit around a common bush afire with God.
We sift the branches with our fingers for blackberries.
We gift the berries to waxwings and fieldfares.
Our gods are Godwits on the moon's magnetic sea.
Snowshoe hares glow like flares on the snowless Sierra.
Ultraviolet rays wake the grammar of leaves.
The sparrowing of spring hedgerows is a second heaven.
The blackbirding dusk is the blush of a feather.
Owls are helved halves of an echoing duet.
The birth of a bird's song is sounded in the shell.
Listen for the snow bunting in a feathering of snow.
A nightingale's song falls over Kfar Aza and Gaza.
As in a day, the nightingale sings. *That day of days.*
The living and the dying are sculpted by scripture.
Your words, words, are gunship helicopters
The time of the Zamir is come, its voice is heard in our land.

A nightingale nests in the thorned crown of your hand.

THE SHYNESS OF THE CROWN

The crowns of trees do not touch each other.
They will not reach because of light and shyness.

They form a canopy and sunlight wakes their shade
as puppet shadows in a shadowplay of leaves.

Branches unfurl their banners. The trees sway in the breeze.
They lean into each other for strength but will not embrace.

The crowns of trees cannot caress or be caressed
lest they fray or fracture. It is a dance of death.

The leaves spill into the only space, above,
endlessly shying endlessly from each other.

I like to think they do this out of love.

THE OATH

I kissed the girl I loved then drove us both
to The Bodleian Library for our first proper date.
Their ancient oath could be sworn in any tongue:
item neque ignem nec flammam in bibliothecam (Latin).
'Choose your language,' said the clerk at Reception.
My girlfriend spoke her vow in *Hiraeth* Welsh.

I asked for Romany. 'Any language but that,'
the clerk tutted. I choked it out in RP
then wrote the Oxford oath in Romany.
I handed the pledge to Security on the door:
Nai anel ándo Bibliyotêka vai luchol vai pàrrâ.
'Offer the vow in this if Travellers ask.'
'I'm sorry, sir. We can't be doing with that.'

I swore to burn the building to the fucking ground,
to smite, deface, and injure every tome.

Fight in speech, not fire, says the book of life.
I held my oath as near to him as a knife:

Wudaréya, parravav tut.

(Romany) -
             'Words will smash the doors down.'

POWER

The Traveller site was running out of food and water.
The shopkeeper had handwritten a sign NO GYPSIES.
Mam couldn't get hold of Sudocrem or nappies.
Her baby cried in the caravan through the night.
The local villagers dobbed her in.
Social Care passed the matter to a caseworker.

A builder fly-tipped a skip on the Traveller site.
The village blamed the Gypsies for the trash.
At the primary school, a teacher called their kids *pikeys*.
Word spread to the playground. It became a killing ground.
There were protests from parents about Travellers in class.
Signs went up around the village saying *F OFF GYPPO FILF*.

The Parish Council complained about the Traveller's site
to the Town Council. Town passed on the complaint
to the District Council. District called in the police.
The police hid until the Traveller dad left for work
then slapped an eviction notice on his caravan.
Mam pleaded with the social worker about their case.

Moan, moan, moan, said the caseworker to her face.
Then they cut off the power to the Traveller site.

COME WRITE ME DOWN

after a Romany song performed by Betsy Smith, 1906

I have a diamond in my eye
and no care in the world despite you.
I'll give you gold and all my pearls
for the Romany families freezing
from dewfall until evening
on their Oxfordshire Traveller sites
in Redbridge Hollow, and Oakley,
at Standlake and Woodhill Lane.
Come write me down, said the singer,
come write me down.

It's not your gold or pearls, my love.
I have no need of either
as I unroll your moneyed mind
and find no heart for your being kind
to the Romany children freezing
from moonrise until morning
on their English Traveller sites
with no water, heat, or light.
Come write me down, said the singer.
Come write me down.

ROMANY READS YOU

The Romany name for Oxford, Lil-Engreskey Gav, means a
town made from books or a town made of readers.

I love the Dr Seussness
of a town made from books.
Oxford spires dreaming on slabs of OEDs
in step-gables of font and paper size.
Hardbacks heaped up as college walls.
Fine print crenelations of Radcliffe Camera.
Oxford commas coursing from clouds.
Oxford sentences clogging the plumbing
under St Giles, Cornmarket, and Carfax.
Chained books in special collections
filing their manacles like Magwitches.
And the pubs, their doors propped wide
with entries from the pages of heaven.
Romany reads the world like a book.
Its tongues are twinned and twined.
It rainbows and unrainbows speech.
Lil-Engreskey Gav also means a town
made of readers, of flesh and blood
scholars flitting in noun-dark dusk.
Romany conjures their college walls,
carves words, weaves worlds,
makes a library a love affair,
leaves a reader alight with lore,
the words now reading her in turn.
Gentiles and gentle readers,
Romany reads you like a book.
Our tongues are twined and twinned.

But you won't believe a word.

ROMANY WORDS
after Edward Thomas's 'Words'

Sorí simensar sí men,
my woven vow:
will you choose me,
you Romany words? –
as balwal blasts
a múro gropalo
or the breshûn
sweetens a kanálo,
their loshalimos
or dukhayimos,
o vuzheyimos la balwaláko –
let me bring the words before you.

I know your art:
you are
a word's warp,
a sentence's harp:
you are sunitóri and suno,
zoralo as bóro,
kamlo as sumnakai,
as máko and kályo,
or a phurano kopúto:
zahárniko as kalo chiriklo,
as the triyandafírya
in the takimos
of mashkár-milásko:

as the Cymru cwtch
of your Hiraeth-wreathed verses,
your English Englyn,
your cynghanedd lusg
versus my cynghanedd sain:
mai phurano than
the Malverns, phurano, -
turned, ternyarel,
po nevo, po nevo:
ternyol as the Severn
del o breshûn:
as the lúmiya, or love.

Spiral me skyward
skylarked with words:
vésalo with vilimos
from Welshêngo-Tem
whose chirikli-ratyáki
have na phakh, –
from Chohawniskey Tem
and Levin-egrisky Tem
and Paub-pawnugo Tem,
through the gajo gavorros, –
where you, Edward Thomas,
stride down May Hill,
your English words singing

from elm top to hedgerow,
and my Romany words ringing
from harebell to whitethroat:
Sorí simensar sí men,
Sorí simensar sí men.
Te avel angel tute.

May the words be before you.

sorí simensar sí men: we are all one; alosarel: choose; wunívar; sometimes; balwal: wind; múro: wall; gropalo: pitted with holes; breshûn: rain; kanálo: sewer; loshalimos: joy; dukhayimos: pain; o vuzheyimos la balwaláko: the whistling of the wind.

sunitóri: dreamer; suno: dream; zoralo: tough; bóro: oak; kamlo: precious; sumnakai: gold; máko: poppies; kályo: corn; phurano: old; kopúto: cloak; zahárniko: sweet; kalo chiriklo: blackbird; triyandafírya: rose; takimos: heat; mashkár-milásko: midsummer; cwch: cuddle (Welsh); hiraeth: land-longing (Welsh); englyn: Welsh verse form; cynghanedd lusg: drag-harmony (Welsh); cynghanedd sain: sound-harmony (Welsh); mai phurano: far older; ternyarel: made new; po nevo: anew; ternyol: young; del o breshûn: after rain; lúmiya: the earth.

vésalo: content; vilimos: sweetness; Welshêngo Tem: Wales; chirik-li-ratyáki: nightingales; na: no; phakh: wings (there is no verb 'to have' in Romani); Chohawniskey Tem: Lancashire (Witches' country); Levin-egrisky Tem: Kent (Hop country); Paub-pawnugo Tem: Herefordshire (Apple-water country); gajo: non-Romany; gavorros: villages; Te avel angel tute: May this be before you.

THE LAST WORD MY GRANDMOTHER SPOKE

for A.B. Jackson

Čīoχ ā!—

the Welsh Romani word for *boots*,

its tongue-tied *χ* stumping around
the mulberry bush of meaning.

A firecracker flung into the campfire
to test the wakefulness of listeners.

Boots! my grandmother would thunder,
listening keenly to the lightning around her.

Go on! What was the last word I spoke?
she growled, glaring into the fire's smoke.

Clutter-tongued, story-slowed, we stuttered
Boots! nana, we are wide awake!

We are still listening, good mother.   *χ*

Čīoχā: boots

At an academic conference I gave a paper
on Romany language. I spoke of its leopard-leap
of dialects: from branch to branch
of Sanskrit, Anglo-Saxon, and Romance;
the open purse of Romany loan words
given and received in kind, and kindness.

How the words galloped, untethered
and language leapt under their hooves.
Why nouns grew spry and spring-heeled
and verbs kicked off, words which Travellers
might ride, or hide behind from hard law,
gajos, or the poisoned pens of parliament.

I spoke all this poetic stuff as prose.
Then I leaned out of art and said, 'My friends,
when police come for Travellers, we move on.
Language shows who we are, and it is better
to be invisible. But spoken language moves
like meltwater under ice. Speech thaws into life.'

There was cold applause. A door whined open.
Catering trundled in, clattering trays
to hurry us along to Q&A.
A young lecturer raised his hand, saying:
What is the point of listening to this trash?
Nobody spoke or spoke up. Tea was served.

Gajo: non-Romany person

DREAMING IN ROMANY, WAKING IN ENGLISH

Ándo suno símas andre bilayimos ai pàrrâ.
Zhivindíl-pe andre breshûn ai skrúma.

I dream in ice and fire.
I wake in rain and ash.

A MIRROR HURLED AT THE WORLD

Do you know Romany names? The braided stories
of their syllables, the words cantering like Camargues

in a river? To rokker their honour is to ride through risk,
in the undertow of their hooved tromayimos.

The women of our camp stride between hedgerows
to your town with brimming baskets, voices low and proud.

Each of the women's names is a chiriklo:
a lòlochìrillo, a ràrtigìllichal, a kàulochìrilo.

The stars are pegged out by the diminatsára.
The night has washed white the sheet of sky.

Every world is wrung out in the wind.
The children stream between the vardos, singing.

The women of our camp stride in their winters and summers.
Their skin is blossom, their eyes pârrâló as flowers.

They are chikalo and zuralo with washing their horses,
scrubbing buriyátsa from horse hooves, lugging wúzho pai

along dual carriageways while HGVs blare and snarl,
whirlpooling their skirts in the wake of wheels.

The women of our camp stride through the ginnels
of your town with baskets of pegs and heather-sprigs.

Esmerelda Hystead. Luminitsa Walker. Kibariye Kabanova.
Pattin Miskin. Yoska Small. Mermeyi Pesha.

Every Romany name is a gledála.
Every story is a mirror hurled at your world.

rokker: speak of; **tromayimos:** threat; **chiriklo:** bird; **lòlochìrillo:** redpoll; **ràrtigìllichal:** nightingale; **kàulochìrilo:** blackbird; **diminatsára:** morning star; **vardo:** caravan; **pârrâló:** aflame; **chikalo:** mud-spattered; **zuralo:** strong; **buriyátsa:** fungus (thrush); **wúzho pai:** drinking water; **gledála:** reflection.

ESMERELDA HYSTEAD

I have washed my bairns in a clanking tin bath,
with pai from the rusty standpipe, sweetened

to tepid by the Calor's blue flame. *Gràdh mo chridhe.*
How they flapped their wings in water, my angels,

their unclad limbs finger-tipping the night.
I plushed them in their Pampers and onesies.

I snuggled them in their knitted blue baby blankets.
I tucked them up in their one cradle like twined fates

sailing the kalisfériya in a crate of bones.
Rive open, ryat, and let them pass, poor bairns,

between spars of space like the children of Del.
Take them in passion, not vengeance for my flaws.

This was my prayer over my huddled babies.
I lifted their tin bath with its lolling water

and christened my boots with the slosh,
scouring my soles with a dandêngi-wûrtza.

The lanes are grimed with cowshit, trenched by tractors.
Lord, I have slogged this dromorro to death.

Where can I find the way where my vardo's wheels
climb clean and true along the tracks of stars?

The planets spin like sugar lumps in my char
burned beneath by boiling it smoky on embers.

The stars spill like pennies kicked from a placky kuchi
by the gajo who passed me on the pavement where I begged all day.

pai: water; **gràdh mo chridhe**: darling of my heart (Scots Gaelic); **kalis-**
fériya: netherworld; **ryat**: night; **Del**: God; **dandêngi-wûrtza**: tooth-
brush; **dromorro**: path; **vardo**: caravan; **char**: tea; **placky**: plastic; **kuchi**:
cup; **gajo**: non-Romany.

The spittle of the market traders spatters my coat.
I sop my mui and sing. The shopkeepers stare daggers.

They back into their doorways like calves in a barn
when the grastêngo swings by with his stun-gun.

Not one has the bollocks to block me. A nation
of tradesmen on speed-dial to the shingale.

The gavvers kettle the Travellers on the market square.
The locals stand by gawking, piss-taking.

A roundup of Gyppos was what Ingerland voted for!
"Suspicion of behaviour likely to cause harassment, alarm, or distress."

These days, even suspicion can snatch you from the streets -
one phone call from a rasísto roused up to gibe Gypsies.

'What is it, sir, are you "distressed", "alarmed"? Or just "suspicious"?'
Officer, he were looking at me funny, and he talks forrin.

I thought we voted to send that lot back where they came from.
And the soft-brained sod pulls the Community Trigger.

A rai-baro logs the stat. The charge sheet states the case.
But the gavver has nothing on me but my race.

I pity the poor pênziyáko. An ashaval through his heart.
His gobbed-up good old days and Airfix spitfire fights.

He shudders like a shoshoi at the baxtalo of Gypsies.
I don't want no grief. Be orf or I'm calling the police.

Serf to his daral, he squanders his pakivime.
Dust, dust, dust: the tread of the trashalo.

mui: face; **grastêngo**: knackerman; **shingale**: police; **gavvers**: police officers; **rasísto**: racist; **rai-baro**: senior police officer; **pênziyáko**: pensioner; **ashaval**: deadlock; **shoshoi**: rabbit; **baxtalo**: greeting; **daral**: fear; **pakivime**: respect/honour; **trashalo**: fearful.

The paramichyári struts the stage of an arts festival.
He pockets a fee that could feed my kids for a sezóno.

My sons are wagging off school because big lads bully them,
calling them pikies, making their lives paklano.

'Mrs. Kabanova, we've had a few complaints,' says a teacher.
The support worker from the council calls by.

'I'm here to help you,' she says. 'You're just adding to it,' I say.
She sends me - of all things - a paramichyári.

'Tell me about your life,' he says with a voice like meláiso.
'I can't write for toffee,' I say, 'but I speak for Travellers.

Our language is the harp I play tunes on.'
The storyteller pulls out a voice-recorder.

'I won't nick your words,' he says, in his accent.
'I want to write the truth about Travellers,' he says.

I say, 'The chachimos don't make fancy art.'
'I'd like to bring public awareness to your plight,' he says.

'You can start by hanging out my washing,' I say.
'Here's a híro,' I say. 'My boy came home last month.

I've had enough, he said. *I can't take it, mam.*
He killed himself next day in the woods. Them woods

down by the dóryav where the townies dump their stuff.'
I hang the tsáliya on the line and turn to the paramichyári.

'Go on,' I say. 'I dare you. Tell his story.
Who tells my truth? A storyteller or me?'

paramichyári: storyteller; **sezóno**: season; **paklano**: hellish; **meláiso**: syrup; **chachimos**: truth; **híro**: tale; **dóryav**: river; **tsáliya**: clothes.

PATTIN MISKIN

My name means *patrìn*, an art of leaf and tree
which Roma place as a marker to tell their families

where they've gone, and where they mean to be.
Few can read them, this word-work of the wêrsh,

a letter torn from the pages of leaves,
scrunched into the crannies of a drystone múro

by the lane's corner on the turnpike of the sun
where the pheasant rasps like a rusty hinge at dawn.

Winter rain shreds my words. The hornbooks of bark
rot into lúmiya under the wheel-spray of trucks.

My tongue sheds its shib, my latticed leaf of speech.
I reach out to you, palms grained by graft,

my arms arching to clasp nuthatches and treecreepers.
The pine marten weaves his drey from my hair.

I dreamed in fire and ice. I woke in rain and ash.
I am the patrìn pawed by vryámya. I cannot rise

from where I was dumped, half-hidden under stone
with kicked-up chik choking my throat.

They took my tongue and tráyo, spread-eagled me,
struck the shib from my mouth, raped me by the hedge

while tourist coaches hissed and settled in the layby
and day-trippers gawped at the quaintness of our camp.

They buried me, shallow, in the wushal of the wall.
In the shadow of you all: I, Pattin Miskin, am the message.

patrìn: symbol or signpost left for travellers made from leaves and
twigs; wêrsh: forest; múro: wall; lúmiya: earth; shib: speech or tongue;
skwártsa: bark; vryámya: weather; chik: muck or mud; tráyo: life;
wushal: shadow.

Christmas Day. The dawn is sure and quick and blue.
I toss the xalayimos on the line and place my pot of cyclamen

where it glimmers and grows and drinks the winter light.
The camp is mad with music. The moon's lamp glitters.

A chirikli-ratyás warms up his wintered song.
Boxing Day. My kids skip off at zóri and leg it to the tip,

quick to the queue before the food bankers show up,
to beg the bed-frame that grandfather spied

among the heaven of unwanted things,
the cast-offs and the grown out of. The sorry mess.

The asamos of children smiling over broken bikes,
trodden toys, rain-sodden teddies, plastic play kitchens.

Imagine the endless Christmas of the recycling yard,
its lolloping wonders and rain-splattered relics

of every toy those parents chose and wrapped.
Their love lies open in the landfill of their lives.

I want to make an afterlife of things
to gather gifts under my vardo like eggs

as though my wheeled house were huddled like a hen
over hope's nest, and each day was Christmas Day

for children of the light and of the dark.
The dawn is sure and quick and blue.

I am Yoska Small. My name means gift.
Rubbish, people call it. I call it love.

xalayimos: wet wash; **chirikli-ratyáki**: nightingale; **zóri**: first light; **asamos**: laughter; **vardo**: caravan.

MERMEYI PESHA

I am a caravan. The eye of my door open to the vryámya.
The Travellers douse me with benzína. I am unclean.

I died when my owner died in me. Mermeyi was barely zhívindo
when the Gypsies cut her down and carried her into me.

They laid her on the ponyévi by my stove. Kibariye nursed her.
Esmeralda phoned a dóftoro who didn't show.

Then the shingale swarmed over the site, with nagging notepads
pushing it that one of our own killed her. They did not search me.

I am a caravan. I cradled Mermeyi in my arms through night and day.
I watched her môritimós deepen to dark. I heard her mind warp.

Her husband Jacko worked year-round hauling palettes
to the edgelands of wild England. A baro was Jacko.

Mermeyi married him at fifteen. She loved him like life.
He'd come and go. Spent more time with his truck than his wife.

The truck's my living, he'd say, revving the matóra, showing off.
The next day Jacko would be gone. Trucking was his true love.

You even sleep with that thing, Mermeyi said.
I sleep in it, he shouted. *Same difference,* she cried.

News came that Jacko had another wife. *I won't leave him,*
said Mermeyi, *even though he's lashed me with shame.*

I am a caravan. My walls closed around my darling in the dark.
Luminitsa and Yoska hammered at my wudar.

The moon had washed white the sheets of the day.
The tree where Mermeyi was hanging was yards away.

vryámya: weather; benzína: petrol; zhívindo: conscious; ponyévi: blankets; dóftoro: doctor; shingale: police; môritimós: marriage (of a woman); baro: big man; matóra: engine; wudar: door.

FADO

Mermeyi Pesha. Yoska Small. Pattin Miskin.
Kibariye Kabanova. Luminitsa Walker. Esmerelda Hystead.

Their names are hushed music like a lark before it sings.
Yet you will not greet them, give them a good morning.

You dread their curse, the plague-cross of their frown.
Nothing today! you mouth through your double glazing.

You scorn them because you were born blessed, raised slyer,
blighted by the memory your kin were once striders.

Your fathers roamed the droms of beggared England,
fossicked for shillings in hop fields and hedgerows.

Your mothers rode vardos, dozed beneath tarp.
Home-chained changeling, you sold yourself for scrap.

You forgot you were a sparrowhawk spiralling with the lark.
Your wolfhound wept wolf. You lay down with the lamb.

Hulisto tele a húlyo hai xutildyas le shoshes.
How the eagle swept down to snatch your soul!

Scram to your burrow, fox-frit, frittering years in your *home*.
The paramíchi of your hero mothers stand over you in shame.

Fado: Song of Fate; **droms:** roads; **vardos:** caravans; **Hulisto tele a húlyo hai xutildyas le shoshes**: 'How the eagle swoops down to claim the rabbit'; **paramíchi:** legends.

QUEENIE ROSE MORLEY
in memoriam 1936-2024

Heartbreaker, head turner, Queenie's name
was Gypsy when *Gypsy* was on the stage
and everything in the fifties was coming up roses.

She had a pout that could pull a platoon,
or spur a cavalry charge in a dancehall.
She swanned down the production line

at De Havilland – "home of the Gipsy Moth" -
stealing the hearts of bloke after bloke
with her sway, smile, and the buff of her beehive.

She was sharp, the bosses said, as a pair of scissors
(school had been barred to her by her Pa).
The world at her feet. Men falling at them.

Chatted up by duck's-arsed teddy boys
on the Big Dipper at Blackpool Pleasure Beach:
'Seven rides non-stop and no payment, love.'

But she'd a boyfriend in Suez on National Service.
That made those boys back off. RAF. Right handsome.
John flew home to woo her, win her with a spin

on the Waltzer, then a slow waltz at The Mecca.
Brylcreemed, dashing, he seemed to step from a musical.
'I never loved a man,' she wept, 'until I loved your father.'

'Here I am,' said Ma. 'Here we go,' said Dad. 'The rollercoaster.'

LIKE FOR LIKE

Mum's iron rule
when I was a kid.
You broke something,
you replaced it exactly.
As it was. No ifs or buts.
A little hardware shop in Thornton
became a second home,
the old man behind the counter
my searcher and saviour.
'We' - he was several men in one -
'don't have *that* exactly'
he'd say, holding to his lamp
the guilt-wrapped
glittering fragments
of a commemorative China mug,
a smithereened ornament
or the jagged glassy shingle
of a prized decorative window.
'But we have *this*'
he'd add with a flourish,
vanishing like a magician
into his holy of holies,
the back-room where the years
of the twentieth century
lay in store on shelves.
'It may pass for the original,'
he'd say, 'in a certain light.'
And I'd bring it home
and place it
like a pardon

in unbroken space.

A MAN OF HIS TIME

My father at the mercy of his rage:

A perpetrator alternates between
violent, abusive, and apologetic behaviour
and heartfelt promises to change.

As he shouted and shouted, I saw
his face swell to swallow the room
until door and windows were gone.

The way out was a space I made in me.
An ice floe at the polar edge of earth.
I froze inside his flow and held my breath

and waited for him to stop or tire of me,
to sob his way to excuses or self-pity
and leave my room behind him in flames.

'He was just a man,' my mum said, 'of his time.'

MASTERPIECE THEATRE

In times of crisis, we must all decide again and again whom we love. - Frank O'Hara

ACT ONE

When I was ten, I pretended to be terminally ill.
With Dad dead of cancer, I craved attention.
Hospital was a holiday from Dad's slow dying.

I was lanced with lumbar punctures and needles
and flushed out as a fake, but a gutsy one.
I put myself to work to make up for my shame.

Work was better than suicide, so I grasped
whatever my hometown Blackpool threw my way,
became a bingo-caller pulling 14-hour shifts,

then a milk float boy up at 4 and out 4.10,
then a 5-round paperboy. Except for the rain
that job was the best: I cheated monotony

by reading the newspapers. Rain drenched
the papers before I could deliver them.
The newsprint bled blackberry ink on my hands.

I gripped my stained fists at school, too busy
to wash, and spilled fingerprints over my books.
One morning, in the hinterlight before rain

I read a note in a letters page from an American
who had met an Englishman on a London train
and wanted to pick up the conversation.

He offered his address in Port Huron, Michigan,
the home, he bragged, of Thomas Alva Edison.
I wrote to him saying I was not the Englishman.

he shot back like a clarion, *Come to me, kid. I'll pay
for everything*. He posted a plane ticket. I flew out
to a man I knew only through an address.

When I touched down in Detroit, I clutched the one
photo I had, and the American sprang out of it.
He showed off my English accent to his neighbours.

Gee, ain't he somethin? The kid sounds like thirty.
Behind his back, knowing his bipolar rages,
his neighbours christened me Masterpiece Theatre,

their little Lancashire Sir Larry Olivier.
I say, old chap, they shouted after me, *what ho! super!*
Out walking with the American, I spied what I thought

were dragged-up bodies in the Saint Clair River.
Icebergs, he growled, *they calve upriver.*
Next day he was sobbing. *Nothing, kid, say nothing.*

The American was sliding into a great lake of himself,
his marriage was an ice floe flowing and fissuring
down the Saint Clair. I was suddenly spare.

He said, *Kid, if you moved out and holed up with
that wild son of mine, well, you'd be good for him.
Time he settled down, and he could practise child-rearing.*

I lobbed a softball to and from The American.
The calfskin glove felt cowardly.
My palm stank of his son.

A house-tamed hippy, his faux-feral boy –
drew the sunlight out, they said, *in everyone* –
hiking deer-trails, 'teaching' me to swim

by drowning me in the creek at Kawkawlin.
Stars flared across his windscreen as we drove,
with tornadoes roiling and flailing their gyroscopes

on the highway between Saginaw and Detroit.
The son eyed me through the half-light
of his pick-up as if he were about to chance

a murder confession. *Boy, you're a game to him.*
Truth is you're trying to be some other father's kid.
I remember how he placed me on the long-haul

to Manchester, smiling and laughing as he strode
from Departures: *Fare thee well, Masterpiece Theatre.*
To thy own self be true! Changeover at JFK,

I bluffed my way to the exit—Manhattan
carved from cloud. Clouds calving
like icebergs from skyscrapers.

I was caught by a kindness of stewardesses,
pushed into a seat on the long-haul to Manchester.
Stars flared in the night sky over the Atlantic.

When I got back home, Ma decrypted
my airmail pad with a blunt pencil.
My letter to The American pleading to return.

I'd *betrayed her*, she cried.
Ma performed to her invisible theatre.
Go! she sobbed, *Go back to America!*

You should be ashamed of yourself.
But my heart leapt up even as I stood
outside of myself, celled in the self I hid.

I wanted blackout on that stage of hers,
trip the trapdoor and hang myself through it
to make up for my shame. I slammed

my bedroom door and read Frank O'Hara:
'I love you. I love you, but I'm turning to my verses
and my heart is closing like a fist.'

Ink bled from my fists until morning.
Dawn shook the compass and pointed me west.
A world elsewhere without mothers

and fathers. I forced the hasps of its door,
sleeping out under stars among sand-dunes
and marram of an imagined Shiawassee.

The Irish Sea drew me to the landfalls
and landing lights of Lancashire sunsets.
Raw sewers fretted with drain-flies and sanderlings.

Low tide, loose-limbed, sprawled to the scum-lines.
I stepped to the ebb to be closer to you, America.
I drowned the one photo I had of the American.

Everybody believes a nice boy like me.
I clutch the Juvenile court witness box.
I hold a book and swear to tell the truth.
I move my mouth to say what I must say.
What is my name. My date of birth.
Where I was on the night of the day.

I was at home. My brother was with me.
I was with him on the night of the day.
He did not leave my side the whole evening.
We went to our beds. I read till eleven.
My mum came home before midnight.
She told my brother what a great job he'd done.

I was at home. My brother was not with me.
He left me alone the whole evening.
I went to bed on my own. I read till one.
My brother clattered in, pissed.
He boasted about a job he'd done
then stashed the stolen goods in the loft.

I perjured myself. The case was dismissed.
I'd held the book, sworn to tell the truth,
clutched the Juvenile court witness box
and looked the judge in the eye and lied.
Nice one, my brother smirked, and left.
Everybody believed a nice boy, except me.

CRAVED

The acronym *C.R.A.V.E.D.* classifies burglary.
The goods you choose to steal and why.
Concealable. Removable. Available.
Valuable. Enjoyable. Disposable.
House burglars swipe cash, jewellery,
passports, IDs, plasma TVs.
Shoplifting is booze, cigs, and the like.
Mums nicking nappies and formula milk.
With vehicles, it's joyriding or engine parts,
fencing them, then torching the cars.
My brother just craved *stuff*. He snouted cash.
It didn't pay for him to be best in class.
It worked for him to be *crim*.
What worked was that craving in him.
To steal and sell half-inched objects,
filch and fence those shit-hot products.
Shoulder-surfing old dears at ATMs.
Twocking Toyotas. Boosting them.
Craved. That was Home Office spin
for the game I found my brother in
and why, through the slips, I dobbed him in.
I grassed because he did me over,
chucked the blame and dived for cover.
He was arrested for a job. He told them
I was there too. A brother in crime.
He'd fooled me into following him
out of bastard trust. I was his alibi.
With one fat fib, he flattened me into a lie.
Locked the door on life and tossed the key.
What worked in me was the craving to be free.
He's the liar, I told the coppers, *I wasn't there*.
Save yourself, said the grasshopper to the hare.

My brother did his time and came out a stranger.

YOU ARE NOW DEATH-SPECTATING

My sons are lethal video gamers.
They chase and shoot my character when I play.
I used to let them kill me out of fun
when they were young, and I was young with them.
I thought that I was gifting them a chance
to win against the odds of experience.

Then I'm sniped and killed with a one-shot skill
and locked outside the game, helpless, watching
their action from a glitched perspective,
an outer space adjacent to the place
of the remaining gameplay in real time:
their running characters viewed from below,
their synced cries, the chatter of their voices.

A half-world where the programming ran out
and the stage of play unravelled into fractals.
You're out of the game, but in it still.
You are death-spectating, your status says.
Ten slow seconds of nothingness before
a second chance to get back in the game.
Your life respawns across their flickering screen.

MIST NETS ON THE LAKE ISLE OF INNISFREE

I wake in my tent to the thrum of linnets
on a morning of insect wings and glimmer,

the mist melting over a mirror of water,
and go. I go with my quiver of mist nets.

CORE SAMPLING AT BLEA TARN

I studied Blea Tarn
for its acid rain.
Insects thrive or
perish under restraint.
Rain runs in ghylls
through ignimbrite,
pooling into peaty
vinegarish water.
A glacier spilt into
Great Langdale
then ice isolated
as it split and flowed
towards Windermere.
Blea Tarn was scooped
high with Side Pike
blocking sunrise,
Pike of Blisco
stealing every sunset
from its surface.
Light levels were
like the moon's.
Insects laid low
in the corrie
under slow skies
of an ice age,
in chill dark water,
like tundra.
Then anglers
introduced fish.

Trout, perch, pike
predated pupae.
Instars of midges
wintered beneath
thinned thermoclines
where the tarn
seeped into mountain.
Vortices of midges
swarmed in spring,
mating, ovipositing.
Swallows hit them
like spitfires from the sky.
Trout torpedoed
them from below.
Their eggs and exuviae
wended down
the water column
like little lanterns,
as light slanted
between mountains,
and fish doused
the lamps one by one.
These stories were
written in water.
I read them from
two cylindrical cores
of sediment drawn
from the benthos
of Blea Tarn.

THE ENCHANTRESS OF NUMBER

*Notes A–G on The Analytical Engine Invented by Charles
Babbage by Ada Lovelace, 1843*

A.   She walks through mathematics like light.
      'We will terminate these Notes,' Lovelace writes,

B.   'by following up in detail the steps
      through which the engine could compute

C.   the Numbers of Bernoulli.' Ada Lovelace
      tracks them through the tables of figures,

D.   her algorithm moving through its meters
      precisely as a pianist playing keys.

E.   'The engine,' she says to Babbage, 'weaves
      algebraical patterns just as the Jacquard

F.   loom weaves flowers and leaves.'
      The Enchantress of Number, her friend calls her.

G.   And all that's best of dark and bright
      meet in the aspect of her mind.

ZYZZYX

Whimsy. If you are not this wasp, that is,
    a polka-dot predator of skipper flies,
        a zodiac of zoom.
You will say
the zyzzyx is all dictionary,

zithering a zero-sum of zeds
    to lock horns onomatopoeically
        with the tropic weevil
zyzzyva.
The last word in the OED.

Whimsy, maybe, in wording
    but not to the monospecific zyzzyx! –
        zootaxied to a single
solitary species
in a zugzwang of six legs and letters

through the zoology and zoogeography
    of Chile. *Are you zeddy?* he asks
        with his zoomed-out
proboscis. *Zure,*
he zigzags to himself, *I'm zeddy.*

MIAOW

What sadist shuts a cat
in a steel chamber
with a flask of cyanide
and a Geiger counter?
Who even *thinks* that?
Worlds decay or stay.
Cats sulk through
those states simultaneously
purr-grumpy, all
quantum and hackle,
headbutting cat-flaps,
slinking through a black hole
into backyards of cosmos.
Their mews split atoms.
They pounce on sparrows
of space and time.
There are a trillion stars
visible in the sky at night
but, for a cat, there
is only one cat.
Cats are thieves of night,
or at least of next door's bin.
Each muon in the universe
has kitten ears that shine.
No cat is ever dead.
No mouse will know such luck.
Life tears us into two.

Open the box. Stand back.

A SEWING NEEDLE IN A RAINBOW

*The Magnetic Properties of the Violet Rays of the Solar
Spectrum by Mary Somerville, 1826*

Worlds circle the axis of her needle.
Mary places her prism of flint glass

by the window, slitting sunlight into
seven ribbons. She hides half a sewing

needle under paper and exposes the steel
to ultraviolet light, spinning north and south

poles from the spectrum. 'As you have seen,' she says
to Turner, 'we perceive the operation of a force

which is mixed up with everything that exists in
the heavens or on earth, which pervades every atom,

rules the motions of animate and inanimate beings,
and is as sensible in the descent of a raindrop

as in the falls of Niagara, in the weight
of the air, as in the periods of the moon.'

BEETHOVEN'S YELLOWHAMMER

'dzi-dzi-dzi-dzi' - call of a Yellowhammer

Some birds sing
the notes of their names
like the Hoopoe and Tinkling Cisticola;
or clamour and chatter
like the Kittiwake or Chachalaca.
Some ask you to take them at their word
like the Grouse or the Go Away Bird.

Do birds sound like themselves
to themselves? Since we
named them by their music
what melodies might we hark
from the Monotonous Lark,
the 'Ō'ō
or Satanic Nightjar?

All birds are composed or composing.
Flocks are orchestra, the dawn a chorus,
and the blackbird an artist of dusk.
Mozart's pet starling
whistling the opening bars
of his *allegretto* in Piano Concerto 17.
Gustav Mahler's cuckoos.

The Yellowhammer clinging
to the tree of the world, singing
Yes Yes Yes Yes
in the Prater Park of Vienna,
fluting the first
four notes of the Fifth.
And Beethoven listening.

ODE TO PSYCHE

> *It is the edge separating my tongue from the taste for which*
> *it longs that teaches me what an edge is.*
> *– Anne Carson, Eros the Bittersweet: An Essay*

I see the jet-streams of sky-harps and meteorology.
Owl-calls rhyming between branches of history.

I hear koalas crying in the Black Summers.
The Cerrado soy plantation's razor wires.

The forestial flowcharts of hyphae and passerines.
They compass you about like bees nuzzling nectaries.

I hear winds catch their breath from forest to floret.
I see the world's ends erode through edge effect.

The loggers have fired the understories.
The gorse-pods, rowan buds, and whinberries.

The rivers shall not overflow thee.
The glacier has shrunk to scree.

The riverbed sings no psaltery.
The meltwater is silenced story.

I hear the nightjars' choir in the cathedral of summer.
I see their heathland cindered by a flicked cigar.

God arrowed Absalom while he hung from the oak.
A woodpecker's drill drives life into the bark.

I say: without you, without us, earth will live on.
You say nothing, nothing to let the warm love in.

EMILY BRONTË

Winter spoke to me from outside my window.

Bare earth and branches. Lichen furred with frost.
My breath made ghosts behind me as I strode.

'Strip your blossom,' said winter. 'Let things pass.'

I thought to answer his flowerlessness with words.
To take his ice and snowball it into stones.

But a sycamore sought the slight light of winter
to throw her first leaf into February for a dare.

'Strip their leaves,' said winter. 'Make life bare.'

The forest woke and bloomed; her trees grew green.
'We are, we are,' sang the sycamores to their kin.

Their roots twined their roots and rose as one.
A snowdrop broke through her shade of snow.

The young year yawned. And winter left my window.

DIALECT

Evening froze to a night nailed with stars.
I watched a birdbox fill with flying words
fleeing the chill by bundling in on each other.

I took the box from its hook and prised its lid
and shook the lives of language out of it
festooning my table with wings and feathers,
writhing, fluttering, like a bird made of birds:

Bumbarrel, Hedge Mumruffin, Poke Pudding,
Huggen-Muffin, Juffit, Jack-in-a-Bottle,
Feather Poke, Hedge Jug, Prinpriddle,
Ragamuffin, Billy-featherpoke, Puddneypoke,
Bellringer, Nimble Tailor, French Pie,
Long Pod, Bush Oven, and Miller's Thumb.

I tucked them in this box before they woke.

EMMONSAIL'S HEATH IN WINTER

'tsee–tsee–tsee' – flocking call of Long-Tailed Tits

See! See! See! says John Clare to Wisdom Smith
as bumbarrels weave through the blackthorn hedge
pricking out insects like picking stitches
from a tapestry of leaves. 'Their name mocks them,'
says the Gypsy, 'however choice the tongue
that broached it.' 'It has been Englished,' blushes Clare.

'I was born with no name,' says Wisdom, 'like a bird.
I forged wisdom for myself when I found my soul.
Why force a name on a thing until it's whole?'
'I find my soul,' sighs Clare, 'becoming those birds,
flitting and fly-catching with my flock. Necklaced
together on our branch, friend by friend by friend.'

'Heel the ground,' kicks Wisdom, 'and feel the iron
frost. Now hang from little twigs and say that again.'

WISDOM'S WORK

'What work are you at, John?' asks Wisdom Smith
'unless watching a fellow work is work for you?'

Wisdom twists a hazel rod between his fists
and twines it taut. The thing he is making
is fighting him back. 'It has such sap and spring,'
gasps Wisdom, as the rod whips across his hands.

'And summer too,' laughs John Clare. 'If those wands
were progged in mud they would root and grow.'

The Gypsy crouches and fitches a woven skeagh,
kneeing and beating it with a rapping iron.
'This wickerwork is for the river, John.
We stake the weir to sieve for silver elvers.'

Clare daydreams at a cloud of dancing flies.
'What work are poets at?' asks John to the air.

WINTER GNATS

Not Christmas, Halloween, term's end, or New Year
but Dog Day's opposite, the eclipse of months, November,

when all's over yet nothing's done, and nowt's in view,
and winter gnats swarm gladly round a sun-touched yew.

PASSION

I want to thank you.
Few poems do
but you deserve more
even if it takes
the sorry form
of a story or song
or a love letter finally
landing in the right heart.
Love is like that letter
in John Keats's hand
—see here it is, he cries—
as he holds it towards you
across a line of words.
A page is a window.
It is not a stage, although
I have played on it.
Nobody who loves you
wants to leave you.
But we do. As Keats does.
Before your train turns
out of the terminal,
or your cab leaves me
at the kerb, watching you go—
pause. For one moment.
And say to yourself
in the small, hard hours:
thank you for the day coming,
through which you and I go,
alive and invisible.
And say thank you,
thank you to yourself
for making of it a heaven.

There are primroses written across the meadows.
We read them aloud. We listen to primroses.
We see them as much by hearing them. We grow
our primroses without thinking them through.
Primroses are born, then made.
All require pruning. There is nothing to get right
and there are no wrong primroses.
Primroses won't obey you however hard you try.
Accept they live, except to die.

Bring your whole life to bear on your primroses, sure,
although less is more.
Growing primroses is also a process
of not growing them, a path of unlearning
as well as unleashing meadowfuls of primroses.
Meadows full of primroses where, like song,
we began by listening. We strewed our meadows
with light, and the flowers grew
without thinking to themselves how they knew
there is nothing to get right, and nothing wrong.

NOTES

Romany words are pronounced exactly as they appear and are glossed below poems.

'The Mist Net Releases Her Birds': to Sarah Rehm.

'We Make Shearwaters Vomit Bottlecaps': The work of Alex Bond of the Adrift Lab collecting bird data on Lord Howe Island in the Tasman Sea.

'Skylark Song Spiral': *Alauda arvensis* 5-letter field code: SKYLA; Basque: zemuta; Catalan: alosa comuna; Corsican: allodola; Czech: skrivan polní; Danish: himmellærke; Dutch: Veldleeuwerik; Estonian: põldlõoke; Finnish: kiuru; French: alouette de champs; Gaelic: uiseag; German: Feldlerche; Hungarian: mezei pacsirta; Icelandic: sönglævirki; Irish: spéirling; Latvian: lauku cirulis; Lithuanian: dirvinis vieversys; Norwegian: Sanglerke; Polish: skowronek; Portuguese: laverca; Romany: cherêsko gilabayitóri; Scots: Laverock; Scots Gaelic: speur; Slovak: škovránok polný; Slovenian: poljski škrjane; Spanish: Alondra común; Swedish: sånglärka; Welsh: Ehedydd.

'Swans': Caroline Herschel (1750-1848) worked alongside her brother, the astronomer William Herschel. She began to make observations separately in 1782, detecting several astronomical objects between 1783 and 1787, including a periodic comet later named 35P/Herschel-Rigollet.

'The First Book Printed by the Sun': Anna Atkins (1799-1871) was an English botanist and photographer, considered the first person to publish a book illustrated with photographic images.

'Ode to a Nightingale': Zamir (Heb. זָמִיר): Name applied to singing birds of the genus *Luscinia* (nightingales) of which three species are found in Israel. 'The time of the *zamir* is come, and the voice of the turtledove is heard in our land' (*Song of Songs* 2:12). The poem refers to a scientific paper 'Towards a standardised framework for managing lost species' by T. E. Martin, G. C. Bennett, A. Fairbairn, A. O. Mooers. In: *Animal Conservation*, Vol. 26, No. 1, 22.02.2023, p. 29-30.

'Come Write Me Down': Redbridge Hollow, Oakley Wood, Standlake and Woodhill Lane are names of Traveller sites in Oxfordshire. Some lines are adapted from a song, 'O write me down the powers above' performed by the Traveller Betsy Smith in Creech St. Michael in Somerset on 9 August 1906, transcribed by Cecil J. Sharp.

'The Last Word My Grandmother Spoke': Phrases adapted from *The Dialect of the Gypsies of Wales* by John Sampson, 1926. *Čioχā!*: 'Boots!' 'Meaningless exclamation interpolated by narrator in the middle of a folktale to test the wakefulness of the listeners who were expected to respond.'

'Masterpiece Theatre': Epigraph from Frank O'Hara's 'To the Film Industry in Crisis'.

'Craved': Criminal slang: 'shoulder-surfing': stealing personal data by spying over shoulder at ATMs; 'Twocking': taking cars without owner's consent; 'boosting': stealing then selling on; 'through the slips': escape a tight or dangerous situation either through resourcefulness or cooperation with the police.

'The Enchantress of Number': Ada Lovelace (1815–1852) is cited as the first computer programmer. The daughter of Lord Byron and Anne Isabella Milbanke, Lovelace became fascinated by the computing machines devised by Charles Babbage. Her table of formulae, sometimes called the 'first programme', occurs in her paper about Babbage's Analytical Engine.

'Zyzzyx': South American Sand-Wasp.

'A Sewing Needle in a Rainbow': Mary Somerville (1780-1872) began carrying out experiments on magnetism in 1825. In 1826 she presented her paper entitled 'The Magnetic Properties of the Violet Rays of the Solar Spectrum' to the Royal Society.

'Beethoven's Yellowhammer': Beethoven's pupil Carl Czerny claimed of the opening of the Fifth Symphony, 'the little pattern of notes had come to [Beethoven] from a yellowhammer's song heard as he walked in the Prater-park in Vienna.'

'Ode To Psyche': Edge effects are changes in population or community structures that occur at the boundary of two or more habitats. The poem refers to the paper 'Invisible destruction: 38% of remaining Amazon Forest already degraded' by Suzana Camargo, *Mongabay*, 2023, translated by Roverto Cataldo.

ACKNOWLEDGEMENTS

To the following publications where poems first appeared: *The Butcher's Dog, London Review of Books, Long Poem Magazine, Magma, Poetry London, Poetry Review, Stand, Times Literary Supplement, To Coventry by Sun: Poems from Twin Cities* (Nine Arches Press), *Travellers' Times*.

Some poems were broadcast on BBC Radio 4 *Front Row* and BBC Radio 3 *The Verb*.

My thanks to Princeton University Press for permission to use the quotations from Anne Carson's *Eros the Bittersweet: An Essay*.

Thank you to everybody at the BBC's Contains Strong Language project; to Jane Commane and Jonathan Davidson; to Sarah Rehm for mist nets; to Yvonne Reddick for snowshoe hares; to Skokholm, Skomer and Bardsey Island for bird reports; to John McAuliffe, Michael Schmidt and Andrew Latimer at Carcanet Press; and to Warwick University for a period of leave.

To Siobhan Keenan, beloved and first reader; to Edward Keenan Morley for energy and encouragement; and to Gabriel Keenan Morley for geography and birding.